Triumphing Through Life's Trials

God's Guiding Hands

Elaine Beverly Robinson Williams

TRIUMPHING THROUGH LIFE'S TRIALS: GOD'S GUIDING HANDS

Dedication

This book is dedicated to anyone who reads it and finds inspiration

Acknowledgment

I WANT TO EXPRESS MY gratitude and appreciation to the writers of this book for dedicating their time and talent to create such a valuable resource. Without your contributions, this project would not have been possible.

About the Author

ELAINE IS THE WELL-known author of the book Reflections. She is a fast learner and enjoys helping the poor, homeless, and needy. I was born in Kingston, Jamaica, on May 5th to Alphonso C. Robinson and Lena Ellis Robinson. I was the third-to-last girl among my ten siblings – five brothers and four sisters.

Chapter 1: Introduction

"Thou you have made me see troubles, many, and bitter, you will restore my life,"

-Psalm 71:20

MY JOURNEY THROUGH life has been a rollercoaster of experiences, and I stand here today as a living testament to the relentless grace of God. As I reflect upon Psalm 71:20, I am reminded of the countless storms, trials, and tribulations I have weathered with God's presence by my side.

There have been moments when the challenges seemed impossible, like waves crashing against a fragile boat. Yet, whenever I found myself on the verge of pain, God's hand guided me through the storm. I have truly understood the depth of God's love and compassion in these trying times. Through them, I have witnessed firsthand the transformative impact of God's intervention. There were moments when the weight of troubles seemed too heavy to bear when life's challenges threatened to overwhelm me. But in those darkest hours, God's presence shone brightly, illuminating the path before me.

One particular instance stands out as a testament to God's miraculous restoration. I faced some near-death experiences that shook me to my core. In the face of mortality, I was reminded of the fragility of life and the fleeting nature of my existence. But in that moment of vulnerability, God revealed His sovereignty. He stepped in and commanded death to behave, breathing life into me. It was a moment of divine intervention, a testament to His limitless power and the depth of His love for His children.

Through it all, I have come to recognize God as a healer and a friend who walks beside me in every trial. He's the Lord who reigns over every circumstance. His restoration has been my anchor, a source of strength that defies human understanding. Each step of this journey has been a testament to His faithfulness, a reminder that He is the ultimate author of my story.

As I stand here today, a living testimony to the miracles of God's restoration, I am humbled by the realization that my life is a canvas upon which He continues to paint. The troubles I have faced are but an opening to the triumphant symphony of His grace. I am living proof of the fact that God's restoration knows no bounds – it is a force that transcends time, space, and circumstance.

The profound purpose guided me to write down the chapters of my life and share my journey. This book is more than just words on paper; it is my testimony to the faithfulness of God, a source of hope for those uncertain about their path in life. I wrote it intending to provide a ray of light to those who are struggling and reveal God's miraculous hands upon my life. For those in the darkness, you may believe in His power and come to know Him as your personal Savior. Life is full of ups and downs, moments of happiness and sadness, triumphs and failures. It's common to feel lost and wonder about the significance of our experiences. However, I want this book to remind readers that God's love and presence never falter, even during the most challenging times.

This book aims to provide guidance, encouragement, and inspiration. I want to reach out to those facing challenges, doubts, or hardships and remind them that they are not alone. God's love has the power to transform our trials into triumphs.

Another reason for writing this book is to honor the lessons learned throughout my journey. Each chapter and experience has contributed to my life, shaping me into the person I am today. By sharing my story, I hope to pay homage to the wisdom gained from both moments of joy and moments of suffering. It is my way of acknowledging that every step, every twist, and turn has been a stepping stone toward growth and understanding.

Over the past 44 years, God has been with me every step of the way. His hands have always guided, protected, and led me. I've had moments of making mistakes, revealing that I'm not perfect. But I know God's love is determined, and I'm committed to Him.

I want to be honest: As children, we've made mistakes and done things that weren't right. But I have admitted to my faults and failures, repented my sins, and asked God for forgiveness. I don't want to turn away from Him or close my heart to His love. I desire to keep growing, learning, and sharing the love that God has shown me.

So here I am, sharing my story. I'm not looking back, and I'm not giving up. I want my life to reflect God's goodness and love. I want to keep moving forward, staying true to the path God has laid out for me. My journey is one of faith, hope, and a deep connection with the One who has held my hand all along. What is God? Who is He? These questions have echoed in the hearts of many throughout history, and my journey has led me to a deeper understanding of the Creator and His power in our lives.

God is the ultimate Creator – the force behind the universe's design, the source of all life, and the guiding hand that shapes our destinies. He is the beginning and the end, the alpha and omega. Through the beauty of nature, the complexity of the human body, and the mysteries of the cosmos, we catch a glimpse of God's majestic craftsmanship.

Believing in God is like embarking on a journey upwards and beyond, leading us to greater heights of purpose, fulfillment, and connection. Just as a seedling reaches toward the sun to grow into a mighty tree, our belief in God moves us toward spiritual growth and a deeper understanding of our place in the grand tapestry of existence. We tap into a wellspring of hope, strength, and guidance when we believe in God. It's like having a compass that points us toward the true north, a guiding light that illuminates even the darkest paths. As we anchor our faith in God, we find the courage to face challenges, the wisdom to navigate life's complexities, and the comfort of knowing we are never alone.

Believing in God isn't a guarantee that life will be without struggles. Instead, it equips us with the tools to navigate those struggles with resilience and grace. Similar to how mountain climbers rely on their equipment to ascend steep peaks, our faith in God equips us with the spiritual tools required to conquer challenges and attain greater heights.

Through belief, we cultivate virtues such as love, compassion, and forgiveness - qualities that elevate us and those around us. It's like taking steps on a staircase that leads upwards and toward a better version of ourselves: the Up and Beyond. When we believe in God's love and purpose for our lives, we are empowered to extend that love to others, creating a ripple effect of positive change.

Moreover, belief in God nurtures a sense of awe and wonder, reminding us of the vastness of creation and our place within it. It's like gazing at a starlit sky and realizing the limitless possibilities that lie beyond. Our belief in God opens our hearts to the mysteries of existence, inspiring us to explore, learn, and seek a deeper meaning. Reflecting on my journey, I am reminded that believing in God is not a mere intellectual exercise but a transformative experience that propels us toward a higher plane of existence. It's like launching on a journey of ascent that leads us upwards and beyond the limitations of our earthly realm.

Believing in God can bring a sense of purpose, hope, and a connection to something greater than ourselves. It's like lifting off in a hot air balloon and soaring above life's challenges, gaining a new perspective on the world and the boundless opportunities that await us. Keep this in mind as you move forward, and let it motivate you to embrace all the possibilities that come your way. So, I invite you on a journey with me that encompasses both spiritual and physical realms. Through this journey, you will gain the same wisdom and enlightenment I have attained from God. With unwavering faith and the discipline to persevere, even the most challenging obstacles can be easily overcome.

"They triumphed over him by the blood of the Lamb and by the word of their testimony."

-Revelation 12:1-12

Chapter 2: Early Memories

"And we know that for those who love God, all things work together for good, for those who are called according to his purpose."

-Romans 8:28

MY CHILDHOOD WAS FAIRLY decent, although my parents separated when I was three years old, and my father, and my cousin raised me. A year later, he remarried, and I lived with my stepmom and father for nine years until I turned 13. It's as if God had plans for me even before I was born. When I was just nine years old, I felt a special calling from God. I started teaching Sunday School at a Methodist Church in Jamaica. I didn't fully understand how the Holy Ghost worked back then, but I listened to God's voice and did what He wanted. And you know what? God blessed me for being obedient.

When I turned thirteen, a significant change happened. I moved to the United States with four of my sisters. We came to live with our mom, who was already living in Los Angeles, California. Traveling from one country to a new state felt like a whole new world.

Growing up, my family had strict rules. Going to church was a must – no ifs or buts about it. After finishing high school at eighteen, something extraordinary happened to me. I chose to accept Jesus Christ as my Savior. It was like a turning point in my life, a decision that marked the beginning of my journey with God.

From the first steps of my journey, it was evident that a higher power was at work, guiding and shaping my path. As I look back on my life, I am reminded of the presence of God, a constant companion who has walked with me through every season, challenge, and triumph.

Childhood is a time of innocence and wonder when the world is seen through eyes untainted by the complexities of adulthood. Within this purity, I first recognized the subtle whispers of divine guidance. Even as a child, I could sense that I was not alone on this journey.

God's hand was there as I navigated the landscapes of early life, gently steering me away from harm and leading me toward experiences that would shape my character. It was a presence felt in the warmth of a hug, the comfort of a whispered prayer, and even in moments of uncertainty, I was held in the embrace of unconditional love.

Throughout my daily life, I have noticed a subtle presence of God's guidance that seems to have woven itself into the fabric of my experiences. Whether through the games I play or the stories I hear, I have felt a gentle nudge toward the path that was meant for me. It feels like the Creator has placed signposts to keep me on track and aligned me with His purpose.

In the innocence of childhood, I might not have fully grasped the magnitude of God's presence, but I could feel His touch in the minor details. Looking back, I realize that every step, every stumble, was part of a greater plan staged by the One who knew me before I even took my first breath was evident.

This chapter is a journey back in time, reflecting on the moments when God's hand was most evident in my early years. It explores how divine guidance subtly shaped my choices, interactions, and understanding of the world. It is a testament to the truth that, from childhood onward, I have been held by a loving Creator who has guided me with care.

It's wonderful to recall the stories of our childhood, especially those that remind us of God's presence through happy memories, our natural curiosity, the love we received from family, and the bonds of friendship.

When I was twelve years old, a seemingly innocent request from my stepmother, Julie Rodney, turned into a trial that would have a lasting impact on me. She asked me to cool down a pot, but I misunderstood and tried to cool down a pressure cooker instead. As a young person, I did not know this kitchen tool.

TRIUMPHING THROUGH LIFE'S TRIALS: GOD'S GUIDING HANDS

As I opened the lid, scorching steam burned my face and left behind a painful reminder. The searing pain was accompanied by confusion. I couldn't fully grasp the gravity of the situation. With a young mind's instinct, I wiped my face with a towel that peeled away the facial skin to stop the stinging pain. The accident left me with a burn on my face and a scar remaining on my left shoulder, a mark that would accompany me through a crucial phase of growing up.

The physical pain was just one aspect. The emotional aftermath truly tested my spirit. The burn kept me away from school for a while. The walls of my home replaced the faces of my peers. The kitchen became off-limits to me. I was banned from a space that had been a part of my daily routine.

In those days of isolation, I was kept from attending Excelsior High School, where a subtle strength emerged: power from an unexpected source. It was as if God's presence became more real, offering comfort and guidance. When the world felt distant and confusing, I found comfort in believing that a guiding hand was leading me through this ordeal.

The accident taught me a lesson not just about the dangers of pressure cookers but about the power of resilience and the grace of God. While the scar on my shoulder remains a visible testament to that incident, it also stands as a reminder of the strength I discovered within myself.

Through my family and friends' support and the unspoken prayers that surrounded me, I realized that I was not alone. God was working through those around me, offering healing for my body and strength for my spirit. During those difficult days, I learned to lean on my faith and trust that God's plan was unfolding, even in the midst of adversity.

Reflecting on how the burn on my face peeled off as I hurriedly wiped away the hot, steamed, stingy, I was afraid that my face wouldn't stop burning. I realize it was more than just a physical scar. It symbolized strength and how God's presence can shine through even the darkest moments. Despite keeping me out of school and away from the kitchen, the incident became a turning point of growth in my life. It taught me that God's strength can carry us through, even in our weakest moments.

I understood that God's love was the ultimate source of comfort during my healing process. It was a love that stayed with me through the pain and guided me toward a deeper understanding of myself and the world around me. What was once a source of hardship transformed into a wellspring of resilience and a reminder of God's presence? This experience showcased the transformative power of faith, turning a painful experience into a testament of strength. Through this journey, I discovered that despite adversity, God's light shines brightest, illuminating the path of healing, hope, and enduring faith.

My school days were marked by a thirst for knowledge and a genuine enthusiasm for learning. I vividly recall the classroom moments when I immersed myself in books, diligently absorbing every lesson. I was a diligent student, always striving to excel and understand the subjects at hand. Causing trouble wasn't in my nature, as I preferred to channel my energy into academics and personal growth.

In those early years, my only notable altercation was a fleeting encounter with a fellow student who fought me on the sidewalk after school. The teacher and my father disciplined me. It's a memory that holds little significance now, a blip in the grand scheme of things. My focus remained on my studies, driven by a desire to do well and make the most of my educational journey.

High school introduced me to a new avenue of self-expression: music. Joining the school band as a flute player allowed me to explore a creative outlet that resonated deeply with me. I dedicated myself to the band, enthusiastically attending games, parades, and performances. The band became a second family, where my passion for music flourished, and some friendships took root.

While high school promised new experiences, it also came with its fair share of challenges. I wasn't exactly the most popular student, and some interactions were met with less warmth than I had hoped. I remember those days in Physical Education, standing among classmates as teams were chosen for tennis and volleyball matches. Being picked last stung, but through the game itself, I found my way to form some connections.

Tennis and volleyball, it turned out, were a bridge to forging new friendships. As I stepped onto the court, my skills spoke louder than any initial judgments. With each swing of the racket, I earned the respect of my peers and slowly found my place among them. It was a valuable lesson – true bonds are formed through shared experiences and the willingness to step outside of my comfort zone.

During these high school years, I profoundly encountered God's teachings. As I navigated the ups and downs, I began understanding the principles of kindness, forgiveness, and valuing every individual. My journey through school reflected these teachings, which led me to embrace learning, cherish friendships, and seek understanding even in the face of challenges.

During high school, I experienced a new chapter in my life when I met my first boyfriend, Curtis Carter, then Bruce Wooden. He became a significant part of my world and a companion in my journey through adolescence. Alongside Curtis and Bruce, I formed unforgettable friendships with people like Doreen and Regina Brown. These relationships were not mere coincidences but were orchestrated by God to help me connect and grow. Bruce Wooden took another woman to the high school prom, and we fell out. I was mad at him; I was a pregnant teenager, miscarried before graduation, and we separated after high school. I reconnected in later years, became pregnant again by Bruce, the baby was born, and he died at six months old at the babysitter.

It's comforting to know that we are never alone as we journey through life. God is constantly by our side, regardless of where we go or what we do. Even if we're not actively seeking His presence, He's always working behind the scenes to orchestrate situations and introduce people into our lives who can teach us important lessons.

Think about it. Have you ever felt a nudge in a certain direction, as if a gentle hand guided you? That's God's influence, gently guiding us toward the best possible outcomes. He watches over us, even when we are unaware of it.

Have you ever had a friend come into your life just when you needed them the most? That's not just a coincidence; it's a result of God's careful planning. He knows what we need and provides for us in unexpected and beautiful ways. Similarly, have you ever felt that inexplicable sense of comfort that you're not alone, even in the darkest moments? That's the presence of God, making you feel His love and care. God wants us to know He is there, offering solace and strength in times of need.

Life is full of twists and turns, ups and downs. We may find ourselves in situations we never anticipated, facing impossible challenges. It's important to remember that God is with us in those moments, working behind the scenes to bring about the best possible outcomes.

Even when things don't go as planned, even when we encounter obstacles and setbacks, God is still by our side. He loves us unconditionally, and He has a purpose for everything that happens in our lives. The challenges we face are opportunities for growth, learning, and drawing closer to God.

God is like a loving parent who guides their child through life's challenges. He knows what's best for us and uses every situation to shape us into the best versions of ourselves. Just as a sculptor chisels away at a block of marble to reveal a masterpiece, God uses the circumstances of our lives to shape and mold us into individuals of strength, character, and faith. So, be faithful, like I have been, and experience God the way I have experienced, and life will be way better.

Chapter 3: Siblings

"A new commandment I give to you, that you love one another: just as I have loved you, you also are to love one another. By this all people will know that you are my disciples, if you have love for one another."

-John 13:34-35

MY CHILDHOOD WAS LIKE a vibrant tapestry, woven with diverse experiences that helped me thrive in life. While some moments were delightful, others presented challenges. Yet, every experience contributed to my personal growth and development.

One of the most memorable incidents from my childhood was when I fell off a high wall. On a bright sunny afternoon, my curiosity got the best of me, and I decided to climb the wall that seemed to touch the sky. Unfortunately, I lost my balance, and gravity took over, causing me to fall. The impact was so severe that it dislocated my right shoulder - a painful reminder that even the most innocent of adventures can result in unexpected consequences.

One of my memories that stands out is when I collided with a tree while riding my bike. With the wind blowing through my hair and the excitement of going fast, I didn't see the tree that was in my way. The crash happened suddenly, and I got tangled in branches and felt embarrassed. This experience taught me the valuable lesson of being aware of my surroundings and the consequences that come with not paying attention. Bitter experiences produce my sweet testimony.

Despite challenges, I had moments of pure joy that shone like gems in the sunlight. I remember vividly the day my siblings and I went on a playful adventure, exploring the world's wonders. Laughter filled the air as we took on imaginative quests, creating memories we would treasure forever.

Playing with my siblings reminded me of my fun and carefree nature. During our playful antics, one of my sisters, Victoria, accidentally hit me in the eye as we fought, stripping my clothes off until we landed in the front yard. Although it was a moment of clumsiness, brawling, and ashamedness, we all found it amusing, and it became another treasured memory of our unbreakable bond as siblings. In a separate but equally amusing incident, another sister, Marcia, willfully waved an icepick around, resulting in an injury that directly stabbed me in my arms. This left a physical scarring in my mind, which left a lasting memory in my family's collective stories.

Amidst the mishaps and merriment, my five brothers- Raymond, Junior, Donovan, Donald, Mark, and my four sisters – Carmen, Victoria, Marcia, and Shirley – were my constant companions. Together, we navigated the labyrinth of childhood, sharing in the triumphs, weathering the challenges, and weaving a tapestry of family love that remains unbreakable to this day.

During these events, I reflected on the important lessons I learned from them. When I dislocated my shoulder, I learned to be resilient when faced with unexpected setbacks. The bike collision taught me the value of being aware and learning from my mistakes. Playing with my sisters and brothers reminded me of our strong bonds and the importance of finding joy in unlikely places.

Throughout all of these experiences, I felt a sense of divine guidance. It seemed like someone was always watching over me, protecting me from harm. These events have become a part of who I am today, shaping me into the person I have become. I am grateful for the lessons I learned, the laughter I shared, and the guiding hand that led me through every twist and turn.

Reflecting on my past experiences, I realize that the scars and bruises on my skin are symbols of the resilience that faith can inspire. Christ's teachings offer a profound perspective - that trials and tribulations are opportunities for growth, learning, and drawing closer to Him. His love is a soothing balm that gently mends our wounds and guides us toward healing during life's challenges.

TRIUMPHING THROUGH LIFE'S TRIALS: GOD'S GUIDING HANDS

My childhood memories have a mix of hurt and healing, pain and laughter, challenges and triumphs. However, faith was the common thread throughout it all. Even in discomfort, Christ's love was a constant presence that offered solace, strength, and the reassurance that no wound was too deep for His healing touch.

These memories fill me with a profound sense of gratitude. I am grateful for the lessons learned, the growth that emerged from the pain, and the unwavering faith that carried me through. The incidents that once hurt me have become reminders of the power of Christ's love - a love that transforms wounds into scars, challenges into stepping stones, and pain into purpose.

Christ's presence is a thread that weaves through every experience, connecting us to a deeper understanding of His grace. Even in the hurt and challenges, a divine light guides us toward healing, laughter, and embracing a faith that never wavers.

Some people come into our lives and make a lasting impact on us. Their presence shapes our experiences and creates a bond of love that withstands distance and time. My cousin, Sister Daphny Grant, is one of these special people. She has been a constant source of guidance and support, reminding me of the strength and importance of family.

My cousin, Sister Daphny Joan Grant, entered and became more than just a family member at a crucial time. She assumed the role of a mother figure and a source of love and support when my mother separated from my Dad. God sent her to support me as I needed a motherly figure to guide and nurture me. She sewed our clothes, combed our hair, cooked, and cleaned the house. Her presence was a healing balm for my broken heart, offering comfort and encouragement when I faced difficult challenges.

Her warm and caring nature filled our home with love from when she arrived. Her nurturing spirit was like that of a mother, and her care was a comforting embrace that helped to ease the emptiness caused by my natural mother's absence. She stood by me, offering guidance, joy, and stability.

Even though my cousin migrated to Canada from the United States when I was thirteen, her influence on me extended beyond the walls of our home. Our bond remained unbreakable despite the physical distance between us. Her departure marked the end of an era but also the beginning of a relationship that would continue to blossom, even across continents.

As the years passed, our paths continued to intersect. My cousin's journey led her to Canada, a land of vast beauty and opportunity. Our meetings became moments of joy, providing us with opportunities to bridge the gap that geography had imposed. Our conversations were filled with laughter, shared memories, and a deep sense of belonging.

One unforgettable memory that stands out is from a spontaneous outing with friends. We ventured out to the picturesque countryside, relishing the breathtaking views and capturing the moment with photographs. Most of my pictures got lost from storage when I became homeless, evicted from my apartment, slept in my car, traveled with spare clothing to change after washing up in gas station restrooms, and stayed in motels/hotels. Despite being unfamiliar with the area, we enjoyed laughing and making memories.

From a faith perspective, I can see the presence of God's hand in the story of our connection. It seems He arranged the timing, the encounters, and the circumstances to ensure our bond remained unbreakable. Through my cousin's presence, I learned about love's power, family's significance, and the beauty of unwavering support.

My cousin's role in my life is a testament to the enduring power of family ties. These ties can stretch across borders and defy time and space constraints. Her constant presence acts as a steady anchor, reminding me that even when circumstances change, our love and connection remain constant.

It becomes clear that family is not defined solely by blood but by the bonds of the heart. My cousin serves as a mother figure, a friend, and a living embodiment of the love God bestows upon us through the gift of family.

Chapter 4: Career Strides

———

"For I know the thoughts that I think toward you, saith the LORD, thoughts of peace, and not of evil, to give you an expected end."

-Jeremiah 29:11

"Thy word is a lamp unto my feet, and a light unto my path."

-Psalms 119:105

MY JOURNEY THROUGH life has been filled with determination, growth, and unexpected adventures. The transitions from school to work and beyond are never easy, but I've tackled them head-on.

My high school graduation was the start of a new chapter, and it's impressive how I balanced part-time work and higher education. I found guidance in Christ through challenges and triumphs as I kept pushing forward.

After bidding farewell to high school, I ventured into work, taking on part-time responsibilities that introduced me to the world of responsibility and independence. It was a time of learning, balancing schedules and responsibilities, and discovering the value of hard work. Amidst the hustle, Christ's presence was like a steady hand, guiding me through each new experience and empowering me to embrace the opportunities ahead.

With a desire for knowledge, I enrolled in a junior college. There, I unexpectedly discovered a lifeguard class that would become a unique chapter of my journey. Through determination and effort, I navigated the challenges of the class and emerged victorious, feeling accomplished.

I decided to pursue a career in nursing because I have a deep-rooted desire to care for others and positively impact their lives. Pursuing higher education was crucial in fulfilling this aspiration, as it empowered me with the knowledge and skills necessary to provide compassionate care.

Upon completing my junior college education at Los Angeles City College, I attended and worked at the California State University of Los Angeles, which quickly became my second home. Through my experiences at California State Los Angeles, I have cultivated a greater sense of purpose and meaning in my life. I am grateful for the opportunities I have had to make a difference in the lives of others.

Amidst the academic pursuits, there were moments of unexpected joy and lightheartedness. I recall when I decided to run for homecoming queen, which led me on a path of courage and self-discovery. Though I may not have claimed the crown, I came in third place. It was a reminder that victory is not always defined by first place but by the journey itself and the growth it inspires.

College was the epitome of knowledge and discovery, where the pursuit of learning takes us to new heights, both academically and personally. As I stepped onto the campus grounds, I carried the lessons and wisdom of my Jamaican education, confident in my abilities. Little did I know the journey ahead would test my limits.

Transitioning from Jamaican schooling, Excelsior High School, to the American educational system was like bridging two worlds. Armed with a foundation of knowledge from Jamaica, I entered California with a sense of intellectual prowess. Yet, as I started with my college courses, I realized that there was a depth of learning that extended beyond my previous experiences. The material was challenging, often stretching beyond the norms I had encountered before. The truth was that I needed to invest extra effort in some areas.

Despite the challenges, I pressed forward, determined to succeed. The school had always been a point of pride for me, where I could showcase my intellect and achieve academic excellence. While I may not have been the top student, my dedication and perseverance propelled me forward, allowing me to earn my Associate's degree in liberal studies. It was a testament to Christ's teachings of hard work and commitment, reminding me that success is a journey that requires continuous effort and faith.

After completing my Associate's degree, I was determined to continue my academic journey and obtain a Bachelor of Science certificate in Health and Nutritional Science. I firmly believe that education is the gateway to unlocking one's full potential, and I was eager to seize every opportunity to expand my knowledge and expertise further. Eventually, my pursuit of knowledge and passion for serving others led me to enroll in medical assistant school. I diligently honed my skills and received extensive training to fulfill my dream of making a difference in people's lives. Then, I ventured on to Los Angeles Trade Technical College to pursue a registered nursing education endeavor. It seemed as though my quest for knowledge was insatiable, an ever-present thirst for growth and improvement. That led me to continue learning about God and how to be an effective leader by enrolling in several Bible Colleges, like the Long Beach Bible College, while I served as a Sunday school teacher. I also enrolled in the International Sunday School Department Cohort 2 studies from December 2022 to March 2023, and I am now enrolled in the Leadership Effective and Advancement Program for Sunday School from July 2023 thru September 2023.

One day, something unexpected happened. While in Registered nursing training at Los Angeles Trade Technical College, I fell down a long set of 25 stairs. It was like a slow-motion tumble; trying to prevent the fall, I held on to the stair handles but ended up at the bottom of the stairs. It ripped off some of my ligaments and strained my muscles, causing me to suffer a back injury with a bulging disk in my neck and lower back. It was a shock, but I remembered what Jesus taught me about being strong and not giving up.

After the fall, I felt sore and shaken, but no one came to help me. I was alone coming from a late Primerica Meeting in the Torrance Business Park, and it was all dark in the evening so that I couldn't see much. I quickly got up and limped to my car. Then, I stood up for a while to take a deep breath. Deep down, I was worried that someone had seen me falling on the floor. It was just a spider and the fact that I was wearing a skirt and torn stockings. I knew it would have turned embarrassing. Even though I was bruised and hurt, I knew Jesus was with me, giving me the courage to keep going. The morning after was when the pain set in.

Getting better was challenging. I suffered sore, stiff muscle aches, torn ligaments, and bulging discs in my neck and lower back, but I had to endure this chronic pain to heal my body. It was tough, but I remembered what Jesus said about not giving up, even when things are hard. Each step forward was like a small victory, and Jesus' words helped me stay strong and keep going.

Looking back, I realize that life is full of surprises, some good and some challenging. The fall from the stairs was a big challenge, but Jesus' love gave me the strength to overcome it. Just like in school, where I worked hard and didn't give up, I applied the same determination to my recovery. Jesus' teachings were like a guiding light, helping me heal and grow, even in tough times.

This incident has taught me that no matter what happens, Jesus is there to help us rise again. Challenges might knock us down, but with Jesus by our side, we can stand up, heal, and become stronger than before.

In my educational journey, Christ's teachings have been the guiding light, illuminating the path through trials and triumph. Each step, each degree earned, and each obstacle overcome serves as a testament to the enduring presence of Christ, a presence that empowers me to embrace growth, pursue excellence, and face adversity with faith.

As I reflect on this chapter, I am reminded that education is not merely a collection of degrees but a journey of transformation and empowerment. God's teachings emphasize that an experience's journey holds greater significance than the final outcome. Jesus often spoke of the lessons learned, the growth achieved, and the faith developed along the way. He encouraged us to focus on the process, perseverance, and transformation within us. Just as a seed grows into a mighty tree, our experiences shape us into stronger, more resilient individuals.

By embracing the journey, we attain our goals, deepen our connection with God, and discover the true essence of living a purposeful and fulfilling life.

Chapter 5: Marriage Life

———

"And the Lord God said, It is not good that the man should be alone; I will make him an help meet for him."

-Genesis 2:18

THE COURTSHIP BEGAN in the church we both attended. We had several outings, even walking at night in the Pasadena Rose Bowl.

He took me shopping at the jewelry store, where he proposed and bought our rings. The wedding was planned three months later, and the ceremony was performed.

I was grateful to God for allowing me to become a bride and experience marriage.

Being grateful and thankful has been a big part of my life. I always remember to thank God for everything He has given me. Even when things were tough, I found reasons to be grateful. It's funny how even the hard times brought me closer to God.

You know, the tough stuff I went through actually helped me become a better person and a stronger Christian. Those hard times were like tools that God used to shape me. And because of my faith, I believe God will reward me for my resilience in this life and the one after.

From this union, I had a beautiful daughter. Becoming a mom is one of the really special parts of my life. Having a daughter is an amazing experience. It's like a bond that's so strong, and it brings so much happiness. We share moments that make life feel special and show us how unique God's creations are.

But life has its twists, and in 1984, I made a decision that changed things. I got married to a man. Now, let me be honest. Looking back, that wasn't my best choice. It turned out that the man I married wasn't the right one for me.

The time I spent married him was a bit tough. We faced a lot of challenges that made things complicated. It was like a storm in my life. But you know what helped me get through? My faith in God. I held onto what I believed in and found strength in God's presence. Even when things were shaky, my faith gave me something solid to hold onto.

Those years of struggle have taught me a lot. They showed me how strong I could be when I leaned on my faith. I learned that even when things seem tough, God is there to help us. He's holding our hand and guiding us, even in the darkest times.

Looking back, I see all the challenging moments were like building blocks. They were shaping me, helping me become a better version of myself. And even though my marriage didn't turn out how I hoped, I can see how my faith made me resilient.

This chapter is about my marriage journey – the ups and the downs. It's not just about the tough times but about how my faith carried me through. I want to show that even when things seem hard, holding onto faith can make all the difference. It's like a light that leads us through the darkest tunnels, reminding us that God's love is always there, guiding us on this life journey.

Life has a way of testing us, pushing us to our limits, and teaching us invaluable lessons. My marriage journey was filled with trials and tribulations that put my faith to the ultimate t est. The storms that raged within the walls of our home unveiled the depths of human cruelty and the power of faith to rise above even the darkest of circumstances.

The fights were loud and fierce, like storms tearing through our lives. It became clear that the man I had married was not the partner I had hoped for. He was an abuser who caused me emotional and physical pain. But two incidents marked the turning point in my resolve to escape the grip of this toxic marriage.

The first was a horrific event that left a lasting mark on my body and soul. It was a day like any other as I went about the mundane task of ironing clothes. Suddenly, out of nowhere, he lunged at me with a hot iron, the scorching metal aimed at my face. Instinctively, I raised my hand to shield myself, and the iron seared the top of my head. The pain was excruciating, but it was the realization that my life was in danger that shook me to the core. At that moment, I knew I had to break free from the chains that bound me to this abusive relationship.

As if the burning pain wasn't enough, another incident that solidified my decision to escape evolved. After giving birth to our daughter, I returned home from the hospital, weakened and vulnerable. But instead of care and support, I was met with an act of violence that sent shockwaves through my already fragile state. He lifted me off the ground and slammed me against the wall, flung me across the room, missing the doorknob. In my weakened state coming from the hospital, the force of the impact stunned me. Several times while pregnant, he would leave me to take the bus as he rode in the car I purchased. When I arrived at church, he pretended as though we were the perfect couple and drove me home.

It's really hard for me to figure out why the abuse happened. It felt like he found joy in hurting me, or maybe he was really upset about something. I married him because he was kind at first, and he attended my church, a potential to be my husband, and you don't marry someone you don't like. Even if you don't like someone, you don't hurt them – you don't hit them, burn them with an iron, or slam them into a wall. It's just not right.

I was so confused about how things went so wrong. I couldn't understand how I ended up with him. He used to be a Christian; he believed in God, and he even went to church. But somehow, all of that seemed to fade away when he hurt me so much.

I used to wonder if maybe he was struggling with something deep inside, something that made him act that way. Or perhaps he felt so frustrated that he took it out on me. I tried to make sense of it all, but it didn't.

It's really tough when someone you thought you knew changes so drastically. It's like the person you once trusted becomes a stranger. And even though he believed in God, his actions didn't match his faith. It left me feeling hurt, confused, and questioning everything.

But through it all, I held onto my own faith. I leaned on God's love and teachings to give me strength and guide me through the confusion. I learned that God's love remains constant even when people let us down. He's there to comfort us, to help us make sense of the things that don't make sense.

The neighbors saw what was happening, and they stepped in to help. They called the police, and when the cops came, they made sure my baby was safe. It was like having guardian angels looking out for us. I called his mom, and she came too. With her help, I gathered my things while the police were there.

After that day, I knew I couldn't stay in that marriage anymore. It was like a dangerous road that could lead to something really bad. I didn't want to go back to that hurtful life. It was like a storm that needed to end.

I tried to understand what went wrong. Maybe he was using drugs, or something else was bothering him. I don't really know for sure. But whatever it was, it made things wild and out of control.

After the divorce in 1986, I faced a new chapter of life as a single mother. It wasn't easy – it was a real struggle. I needed help, and thankfully, church friends came to my aid. They offered me a place to stay, and I also had to rely on welfare, like food stamps and Medical Medicare, to make ends meet. But even with that assistance, providing for me and my daughter on my own was tough. I was evicted from my home, was homeless, had to sleep on the babysitter's floor, lived out of my car, motels, and hotels, walked home, and could not even afford bus fare. Simply unpleasantness.

Being a single mom brought challenges every day. I watched my daughter grow up, go to school, and graduate from high school here. Then she spread her wings and moved away to Georgia, Atlanta. She was on her own, making her own way. She got a job there, but things didn't go as planned. She ended up staying with a friend's mom until she could find her own place.

One of my life's special parts has been becoming a mom and a grandma. Over the past ten years, she's carved out her own path. She became a homeowner and embraced the responsibilities that came with it. And now, she's in North Carolina, living near her Dad. Life has taken her to different places, and she's faced its ups and downs with strength.

Today, my daughter is doing well. She's a mother herself, with a baby born in Georgia and residing in North Carolina. She found a townhouse that suited her needs. Looking back on our journey, as one does, I can see how far we've come. The struggles were real, but they made us stronger. It's a reminder that even in the face of challenges, God's love is always there to guide us, giving us the strength to overcome and thrive.

In those moments of despair, my faith in God became my lifeline. When I had no strength to fight back, I desired guidance from Him. The teachings of Christ echoed in my heart, reminding me that even in the face of darkness, there is a light that can never be extinguished. I found the courage to take a stand, leave the torment behind, and step into a future defined by faith, strength, and resilience.

The journey ahead was not easy, but armed with faith and the support of those who stood by me, I began the process of rebuilding my life. Through therapy, counseling, and the loving embrace of family and friends, I found the healing I so desperately needed. The scars on my body reminded me of the battles I had fought and conquered, but they were also a testament to the power of faith to overcome even the most harrowing of experiences.

Chapter 6: Accident Recalled

―――

"The righteous cry out, and the Lord hears them; he delivers them from all their troubles. The Lord is close to the brokenhearted and saves those who are crushed in spirit."

-Psalm 34:17-18

IN LIFE, SOME MOMENTS test our strength and resilience, moments when we feel like the world is collapsing. These are the times when we often turn to our faith, seeking comfort and guidance.

Two years ago, a car accident changed my life. As I approached a busy four-way intersection, fate took an unexpected turn. The brakes failed, and panic gripped my heart. In a split second, I made a decision that changed my destiny. I swerved toward the sidewalk to avoid disaster, unaware that this choice would lead to divine protection.

The car skidded to the sidewalk and collided with a tree. An iron bar was concealed within that tree. The impact caused my car to flip, leaving me suspended upside down, trapped and helpless. Glass shattered around me, and fear threatened to overwhelm my senses. But even in that chaos, I felt a presence, a calming assurance that I was not alone.

The realization of the narrow escape began to sink in. The tree had acted as a barrier, preventing my car from colliding with the gas station or re-entering the treacherous intersection. Reflecting on the sequence of events, I felt grateful my undeployed airbag spared my neck.

First responders arrived at the chaotic scene, where my car had overturned and became tangled in metal, showing the gravity of the situation. Yet, I clung to the knowledge that divine intervention had spared me from the horrors of disaster.

I believed God's hand had been at work throughout my physical recovery, emotional healing, and rebuilding of shattered confidence. Each step of the journey was a testament to His grace and mercy. The accident became a turning point, a catalyst for reflection and growth. In my darkest hour, surrendering to a higher power gave me strength. The accident reminded me that we are never alone despite life's greatest trials. The intricate tapestry of events that unfolded on that fateful day was a testament to God's unfailing love and protection. Through it all, I learned that even amidst chaos, there is a divine order guiding us through the storms of life.

This incident made me recall my arrival on American soil. I was unaware it would lead me to a profound relationship with faith and a purpose beyond my imagination. My story began in Jamaica, where the seeds of my calling were sown long before I understood their significance.

Baptism symbolized my commitment, a public declaration of my newfound faith. The waters that enveloped me represented a rebirth, a washing away of old doubts and fears. With each droplet that touched my skin, I felt a renewal of purpose, a profound sense of belonging to a greater plan.

In the following years, I felt a calling to serve in ministry as a licensed evangelist and Minister of the gospel of Jesus Christ. I embraced this role with humility and gratitude, recognizing that it was the purpose whispered into my soul long before I fully comprehended its weight.

After experiencing the highs and lows, joys, and challenges of ministry, I have learned that surrendering to God's call is a journey that requires unwavering trust. His wisdom guides each step I take, and every word I share is a testament to His boundless mercy. My story is a testimony to the incredible ways God works, weaving together the threads of our lives to create a tapestry of purpose and meaning.

Looking back, I am humbled by the realization that God's hands were upon me even before I recognized His presence. My journey from Jamaica to the United States, from a young soul teaching Sunday school to a licensed evangelist, is a testament to His faithfulness and the beautiful ways He fulfills His promises.

Life is like a journey with many different paths. Sometimes, these paths can get difficult, and we face problems. It's important to know that these hard times are part of life and don't just happen once. They might make us sad or disappointed, but that doesn't mean we should stop moving forward.

Think of it like this: imagine a bumpy road. We might feel uncomfortable when we drive over bumps, but we don't stop driving. Keep going because we know the bumps won't last forever. In the same way, the tough times we face won't last forever either.

Feeling sad or frustrated is okay when things don't go well. These feelings are like clouds that come and go. They might block the sun for a while, but eventually, the sun will shine again. Feeling these emotions is normal, but we shouldn't let them control us.

Being strong during hard times is like being a tree in a storm. The wind might push and shake the tree, but it doesn't break. We can be like that tree by staying strong and flexible when faced with challenges. Like a tree grows stronger from facing the wind, we can grow stronger from facing our problems.

Remember, tough times are not the end of the story. They are like chapters in a book, and we keep writing our story by moving forward. We can learn from these experiences and become better and stronger. By facing challenges with courage, we show we can overcome and keep going.

After the accident, I found myself in the Trauma Center. It's like a special part of the hospital for hurt people. They did a lot of tests on me, like CAT scans and MRIs, to see what was wrong. It turned out that I had hurt my head, got a broken rib, and twisted my ankle because of what happened with my foot and the car pedals.

The doctors said my head had been injured and my rib was crushed. My foot stuck between the brake and the gas pedal, so the car didn't stop. I don't remember when my car flipped over, but I think it happened thrice. Amazingly, I didn't hit anyone else on the road or crash into another car. I believe God was watching over me that morning, keeping me safe.

I was really out of it when the accident happened. I don't know if they thought I might have died at the scene. But later, when I woke up in the Trauma Center, they checked to see if I had been drinking. I wasn't, though. I was perfectly fine when I left for work that day.

While I was at the hospital, they gave me some medicine and did some things to help me. But I didn't want to stay there too long because they didn't give me any food. They said that if they gave me something hot to drink, I might go into a deep sleep, like a coma. I tried to rest, but they kept waking me up. I was at that Trauma Center all day, and I felt like I was strong enough to return home.

The whole day at the Trauma Center was a blur. They checked me out but didn't keep me there because my injuries weren't too serious. They wanted me to be watched over, though. So, when I finally got back home, I felt a mix of relief and exhaustion.

Before the car accident, there was something else I had to face – breast cancer. Doctors found a lump in my breast, and I had an operation to remove it. Then, I went through chemotherapy and radiation to fight the cancer. It was like dealing with two tough things at once.

When leaving the hospital after the accident, I did my best to act okay. My sister came to get me because my car was wrecked, all bent up. They had to use special tools to open the doors and get me out since the car had flipped over.

Life threw some big challenges my way, but I wasn't about to let them keep me down. Even when things seemed tough, I kept going. It's like taking one step at a time, moving forward no matter what. And with my sister by my side, I knew I wasn't alone in facing these obstacles.

The accident and the battle with cancer were like storms in my life, but I didn't let them define me. Instead, I used them as opportunities to show my strength and determination. Each hurdle I overcame was a small victory that reminded me of the power we have within ourselves to keep pushing forward.

It's been two and a half years since the accident, and I want to be honest with you—I'm not fully recovered yet. I still need a walker to help me get around, and I can't walk for long distances. Sitting too long is also challenging because of my messed-up spinal cord and back.

I have a wheelchair, but I've struggled using it because I don't always have someone to push me around. I didn't want to rely on the wheelchair too much, so I've been trying to walk with my walker. Since the day of the accident until now, there's been progress. Back then, I could barely move. I felt stiff and frozen, and the pain was overwhelming. But now, I can tolerate the pain and keep moving forward.

Every morning, I thank God for giving me another day. I know things could have turned out differently; my car did not explode, airbags did not deploy, I did not crash in the gas station, thank God I did not enter that busy four-way intersection, I thank God the first responders came to my rescue quickly, and I'm grateful for each opportunity to keep going. I have read and seen other reports of similar accidents with my car upside down, that they didn't make it. I am so thankful to God for sparing my life. It's a reminder that life is precious, and I'm determined to make the most of it.

You might be wondering how I managed on my own. Since 2018, I've been living with my sister and her husband. They've been like my guardians, caring for me and helping with daily tasks. My sister has been there every step of the way, cooking for me, ensuring I'm okay, and even helping me with things like bathing and keeping my bathroom clean.

Life has had its challenges, but I'm taking things one day at a time. I'm grateful for the support of my sister and the chance to keep moving forward, no matter how tough things may seem. Each small step is a victory, and I'm determined to keep pushing through, making the most of every moment.

Chapter 7: Divine Love

"Above all, love each other deeply, because love covers over a multitude of sins."

-1 Peter 4:8

THROUGHOUT THE PAGES of this book, my determined relationship with God has been a thread that weaves the fabric of my life. From the very beginning, I have found relief, strength, and support in the arms of my Creator. In this chapter, I invite you to dive deeper into my faith journey and how my relationship with God has shaped every aspect of my existence.

I was introduced to God's boundless love and guidance as a young child. Simple bedtime prayers and conversations with my family about the Creator laid the foundation for my understanding of a higher power. These early interactions planted the seeds of faith that would later blossom into a robust and unbreakable connection.

Life's journey is paved with challenges, and my path was no exception. From mundane struggles to heart-wrenching trials, my faith was a constant companion. When difficulties arose, I turned to God, seeking strength and comfort. Through each hardship, I witnessed the timely arrival of solutions, often in the form of unexpected blessings that eased my burdens.

My relationship with God transcends mere ritual; it's a deeply personal and intimate connection. I found solace in prayer, pouring out my heart and soul to the One who understood my joys and sorrows. In those moments of vulnerability, I felt an overwhelming sense of being heard, a confirmation that I was not alone in my experiences.

Throughout my life, I have faced countless crossroads and pivotal decisions. In these moments of uncertainty, I turned to God for guidance. Through quiet reflection and a willingness to listen, I discerned a guiding voice that directed me toward the path that aligned with my true purpose. No matter how significant, each decision became an opportunity to strengthen my bond with the Divine.

Time and time again, I have witnessed what can only be described as miracles in disguise. From the smallest details to life-altering events, I have been humbled by how God's hand has intervened. These divine interventions often manifested as a helping hand extended by a stranger, a timely phone call, or an unexpected opportunity that paved the way for a brighter future.

Throughout my life, gratitude has been a consistent theme that I deeply cherish. My connection with God has instilled within me a profound appreciation for all the great and small blessings accompanying me on my journey. This appreciation gives me a sense of purpose. I recognize that my life is a divine tapestry woven with intention, and every experience - joyful or difficult - plays a crucial role in my spiritual development.

I want you to understand who God is. God, often understood as the divine Creator and supreme being, is a concept that holds deep significance across various cultures and belief systems. While our understanding of God may vary, the essence of this concept remains a central force in the lives of many.

At its core, the idea of God revolves around the concept of creation. Many people believe that God is the originator of the universe, the source of all life and existence. It's like imagining an artist who skillfully crafts a masterpiece—God is seen as the ultimate Creator who shaped the cosmos and all that inhabits it.

When we talk about God, we often attribute certain qualities to this supreme being. These qualities are often described using words like omnipotent (all-powerful), omniscient (all-knowing), and omnipresent (present everywhere). These characteristics illustrate the idea that God possesses limitless power, knowledge, and presence, transcending the limitations of human understanding. One of the fascinating aspects of God is the belief in a reality beyond the physical realm.

Many people perceive God as existing beyond the confines of time and space, encompassing a spiritual dimension that transcends our earthly experiences. This understanding invites us to consider that while interacting with the tangible world, a more profound, unseen reality connects us to the divine.

TRIUMPHING THROUGH LIFE'S TRIALS: GOD'S GUIDING HANDS

The concept of God often addresses the fundamental human quest for meaning and purpose. Believers find solace in the idea that there is a higher purpose to their lives, guided by a divine plan. God becomes a source of guidance, offering direction and support in navigating life's challenges and uncertainties.

It's important to note that people's views of God can vary widely. Different cultures, religions, and spiritual traditions have their own interpretations and understandings of the divine. Some envision God as a personal being with whom they can have a direct relationship, while others see God as an impersonal force that permeates the universe.

The belief in God often rests on faith—a deep-seated trust and conviction in something that may transcend empirical proof. This faith provides comfort, strength, and a sense of connection to something greater than ourselves. People draw on their faith to find purpose, seek guidance, and navigate the complexities of life. As a concept, God embodies the Creator of all existence, possessing divine qualities beyond human understanding. Believers perceive God as existing beyond the physical realm, offering meaning, purpose, and guidance to those who seek it. While interpretations of God may differ, the core idea of a supreme being remains a powerful force that shapes the lives and beliefs of many.

The Bible presents a striking depiction of the Lord's magnificence and elevated essence. Through its pages, we are presented with an awe-inspiring and affectionate God whose grandeur, might, and steadfastness are evident in the lives of His creations. Let's explore the biblical outlook on the Lord's identity and the boundlessness of His greatness.

He is the Creator of All Things. The Bible opens with a powerful declaration of the Lord's greatness as the Creator of the universe. In the book of Genesis, we read how God spoke the cosmos into existence, bringing forth light, land, sea, and all living creatures. This act of creation reveals His immense power and wisdom as the Master Designer behind the intricate tapestry of life.

"In the beginning, God created the heavens and the earth."

- Genesis 1:1

He is Sovereign and Omnipotent. The Old and New Testaments vividly portray the Lord's sovereignty and omnipotence. He reigns as the supreme ruler over all things, with authority that extends beyond human comprehension. The biblical accounts of miraculous events, such as the parting of the Red Sea and the resurrection of Jesus, underscore His limitless power. In Revelation 22:13, God says,

"I am the Alpha and the Omega, the First and the Last, the Beginning and the End."

He has Unfailing Love and Compassion for us. While the Lord's might is undeniable, His greatness also shines through His boundless love and compassion. The Bible repeatedly emphasizes God's care for His people, depicting Him as a tender shepherd who guides, protects, and provides for His flock. His willingness to forgive and restore, even in the face of human shortcomings, reveals His unparalleled grace. *Psalm 103:8 talks about this by saying,*

"The LORD is compassionate and gracious, slow to anger, abounding in love."

He is Eternal and Unchanging. The Lord's greatness extends beyond the constraints of time and change. He is the eternal "I Am," existing outside past, present, and future boundaries. This timeless nature highlights His constancy and reliability, offering a firm foundation for believers to anchor their faith.

"Jesus Christ is the same yesterday and today and forever."

He is Majestic and Only Worthy of Worship. The Bible paints a majestic portrait of the Lord seated on His heavenly throne, surrounded by angelic hosts proclaiming His holiness. His greatness evokes awe and reverence, inspiring heartfelt worship and adoration from all creation.

"Great is the LORD, and greatly to be praised, and his greatness is unsearchable."

-Psalm 145:3 (KJV)

TRIUMPHING THROUGH LIFE'S TRIALS: GOD'S GUIDING HANDS

The Bible vividly portrays the Lord's magnificence, revealing Him as an unmatched Creator with sovereign rule over all and a source of unwavering love and compassion. It also depicts Him as an eternal, unchanging presence and a majestic recipient of worship. These pages offer insight into His vast nature and deep affection for humanity. We are invited to marvel at the Lord's greatness and respond with genuine gratitude, devotion, and praise.

I, too, stand before you as a flawed individual, well aware of my shortcomings and the mistakes I have made along the way. But within this imperfection lies a transformation journey, where the pursuit of goodness, the glorification of God, and the embrace of redemption have shaped my path.

Realizing one's imperfection can be a humbling experience, a reminder that we are all part of the same intricate design. I have stumbled, faltered, and grappled with the weight of my own mistakes. Yet, within this vulnerability, I have discovered the true essence of being human—learning, growing, and yearning for a higher purpose.

In the face of my imperfections, I felt a call to action—an inner voice urging me to strive for improvement, to reach for the light amidst the shadows. With determination, I embarked on a journey of self-betterment. I recognized that by seeking to better myself, I could contribute to bettering the world around me.

I found strength in my faith. A faith that compelled me to glorify God through selfless acts of service. I reached out to those in need, offering a helping hand, a kind word, and a warm embrace. Each act of kindness was a testament to my commitment to honor the Creator by reflecting His compassion and love.

The path of goodness is not without its challenges, and I faced my share of obstacles. But with every step forward, I felt a sense of alignment with a higher purpose that resonated with the divine blueprint. Each smile I brought to a stranger's face, each moment of ease I offered to a friend, became a testament to the transformative power of goodness.

During moments of solitude, I found consolation in prayer, which was a lifeline connecting my soul with the Divine. I openly shared my flaws in these sacred conversations and strived for forgiveness, guidance, and strength. Knowing that God's mercy is boundless, I poured my heart out with the confidence that He would accept me as I am.

I want you to know that I am not perfect. I am a fellow traveler on this journey we call life. Our imperfections connect us in our shared humanity and allow us to shine with our own unique light. I carry with me the lessons I have learned and the kindness I have received, knowing that redemption is a promise for all of us. It is a beautiful thread woven into the fabric of our lives.

For the love of God, my journey led me to Long Beach, California, where I found inspiration at Victory Outreach. This place became a sanctuary of encouragement and support during a pivotal time, especially after the painful loss of my beloved son, Denzel Wesley Wooden. Within the caring embrace of Victory Outreach, I found the strength to heal and rebuild my life.

Their prayers lifted me through the darkest days, helping me find my way back to a sense of purpose. I embraced a path of repentance, seeking forgiveness for my past mistakes. Immersed in their teachings, I nourished my spirit with the word of God, finding renewed hope and direction.

With the guidance of Victory Outreach, I stepped into active roles within the community. I ventured out to share the message of faith and love, participating in the women's ministry and connecting with fellow singles who shared similar journeys. The bonds I forged here became pillars of strength, reminding me that I was never alone on this path.

As time progressed, Victory Outreach underwent a relocation, and I found myself on a new path again. Pastor Leon Woods extended an invitation, thrusting me into a Sunday school teaching role. This unexpected opportunity challenged me to deepen my understanding and connection with God's teachings.

TRIUMPHING THROUGH LIFE'S TRIALS: GOD'S GUIDING HANDS

My commitment to growth led me to the Long Beach Bible Institute, where I eagerly soaked in wisdom and knowledge. With dedication, I completed a Certificate of Completion, a testament to my studies in Church & Pulpit Etiquette, Altar Worker Ministry, Officiating Formal Weddings & Funerals, Pre-Marital & Post-Marital Counseling, and even courses on recognizing and assisting battered and abused women and children. The Barbara McCoo Lewis School of Missionary Development further enriched my learning journey.

These experiences taught me that my journey reflects God's love and guidance. From the nurturing embrace of Victory Outreach to the challenges and growth at Pastor Leon Woods' side, each step has been a testament to the transformative power of faith. As I stand here, equipped with the knowledge and a heart full of gratitude, I am reminded that my journey is a testimony to God's enduring presence and His ability to lead us through even the most challenging of times.

My journey surely is a testament to the enduring nature of a relationship with God. It is a bond nurtured through prayer, trust, and a belief in His guidance. God's presence has been a constant source of comfort, strength, and inspiration through the highs and lows. My life's story is a testament to the transformative power of faith, reminding us that even in our darkest moments, the light of divine love shines brightly, illuminating our path with hope and purpose.

Chapter 8: Volunteering Work

———

"Whatever you do, work at it with all your heart, as working for the Lord, not for human masters, since you know that you will receive an inheritance from the Lord as a reward. It is the Lord Christ you are serving."

-Colossians 3:23-24

"For I was hungry and you gave me something to eat, I was thirsty and you gave me something to drink, I was a stranger and you invited me in."

-Matthew 25:35

WHEN I DEVOTED MY LIFE to God, my heart was filled with a deep sense of purpose and a strong desire to make both God and the world proud. It was a commitment that went beyond words, motivating me to take action and make a positive impact through volunteer work.

One significant way I channeled my devotion was through prison ministry volunteering. This involved visiting correctional facilities and connecting with inmates, many of whom were seeking a chance for redemption and transformation.

Prison ministry volunteering is a heartfelt endeavor that involves reaching out to incarcerated individuals and offering them emotional and spiritual support within the confines of correctional facilities. Volunteers establish meaningful relationships with inmates through organized visits and group sessions, aiming to provide a positive influence that can contribute to their personal growth and rehabilitation.

These interactions often involve sharing messages of faith, hope, and forgiveness. Volunteers may read from religious texts, pray, and facilitate discussions, encouraging inmates to reflect on their past choices and consider a more positive path forward. Beyond the spiritual aspect, volunteers also provide vital emotional support, creating a safe space where inmates can express their feelings, fears, and aspirations.

One of the core objectives of prison ministry is to offer guidance and mentorship. Volunteers assist inmates in developing life skills, making constructive decisions, and setting achievable goals. Workshops on anger management, conflict resolution, substance abuse recovery, and vocational training are organized to equip inmates with practical tools for personal development.

In addition to workshops, volunteers often engage in creating reentry plans with inmates. These plans outline a roadmap for their successful reintegration into society upon release. By connecting inmates with resources for housing, employment, education, and social services, volunteers help them lay the foundation for a more positive future.

A key aspect of prison ministry is cultivating community within correctional facilities. Volunteers work to foster a supportive environment that encourages inmates to engage in positive activities, build healthy relationships, and envision a life beyond their current circumstances. This sense of belonging can be crucial in motivating inmates to make positive changes in their lives.

Beyond the direct impact on inmates, prison ministry volunteers may also engage in advocacy efforts to raise awareness about issues affecting incarcerated individuals. By sharing their experiences and insights with the broader community, volunteers contribute to discussions surrounding criminal justice reform, rehabilitation, and restorative justice initiatives.

Engaging in prison ministry offers volunteers a unique opportunity to cultivate empathy and deepen their understanding of the challenges those behind bars face. Through these efforts, volunteers bring messages of hope, compassion, and transformation to incarcerated individuals, reminding them that they are not defined by their past mistakes and inspiring them to embrace a brighter future.

As I stepped inside the prison walls, I was met with mixed emotions—compassion, empathy, and a touch of apprehension. The environment was stark, but I felt a strong calling to bring a message of hope to those who might have felt forgotten or abandoned.

During these visits, I engaged in heart-to-heart conversations with the inmates. I listened to their stories, shared passages from the Bible, and offered words of encouragement. Through these interactions, I aimed to remind them of their inherent worth and potential for positive change. I saw the impact of a kind word and a listening ear—how it could brighten their spirits and spark a glimmer of hope. Witnessing their vulnerability and resilience was a humbling experience, and it reinforced my belief in the transformative power of God's love.

Feeding homeless individuals was another way I translated my dedication into action. I joined efforts to nourish those facing the harsh realities of life on the streets. Participating in food distribution events was both eye-opening and heartwarming. As I helped prepare meals and packed food items, I could feel the anticipation and gratitude in the air.

Distributing food and sharing a warm meal with the homeless was a profound experience. It wasn't just about providing sustenance but acknowledging their humanity and letting them know they were seen and valued. The conversations we shared were filled with moments of connection and understanding. As we sat together, I heard stories of resilience and survival, dreams and aspirations. It was a powerful reminder that these individuals possessed a wealth of untapped potential despite their circumstances.

TRIUMPHING THROUGH LIFE'S TRIALS: GOD'S GUIDING HANDS

In both prison ministry and feeding the homeless, I was guided by the teachings of my faith. I saw firsthand how a simple act of kindness could brighten someone's day and offer a glimmer of hope. These experiences became a living testament to my dedication to God and my commitment to embodying His love and compassion in tangible ways. Through these acts of service, I discovered the true meaning of selflessness and the profound impact each individual can have on the lives of others.

Lastly, I would like to share my meaningful experience of visiting nursing homes for prayer. This aspect of my journey has been deeply enriching and has allowed me to extend love and compassion to an often overlooked segment of our society.

Visiting nursing homes for prayer is an opportunity to bring relief, comfort, and spiritual connection to elderly residents. As I entered these care facilities, I was met with an atmosphere that resonated with a mix of emotions—resilience, nostalgia, and a yearning for companionship. These individuals, often confined to their rooms or communal spaces, welcomed the presence of someone who cared, was willing to listen, and was there to share moments of reflection and devotion.

Engaging with the elderly residents was a humbling experience. I engaged in conversations that ranged from sharing life stories to discussing faith and spirituality. I often brought passages from religious texts, uplifting messages, and prayers that resonated with their experiences. The simple act of holding their hands and offering a moment of connection through prayer brought a sense of comfort and reassurance.

Many elderly individuals I met had rich histories and stories to share. Their eyes lit up as they reminisced about their past, and they expressed gratitude for the opportunity to share their thoughts and memories with a willing listener. Through these interactions, I learned the importance of being present at the moment, valuing the wisdom that comes with age, and understanding that each person's journey is unique and worthy of respect.

Praying with the residents was a profoundly moving experience. As we bowed our heads and offered words of gratitude, supplication, and hope, I could feel the energy shift in the room. It was as if a sacred space had been created, where the concerns of the world outside momentarily faded, and a sense of peace enveloped us. These moments of prayer provided spiritual comfort to the residents and left a lasting impact on my heart.

My experience as a volunteer has been outstanding, enriching my life in ways I never thought possible. From prison ministry to feeding people experiencing homelessness, every moment has shown me the transformative power of love and dedication.

You need food to live!

Volunteering work was the food for my soul. I've seen firsthand how a kind word or gesture can impact someone's life, reminding me of the beauty in our shared human experience. Through serving others, I've embodied my faith in action and played a small role in making a positive difference.

This journey has strengthened my belief in positive change and my commitment to spreading kindness wherever life takes me. I've learned that giving gives us far more than we could ever imagine.

Chapter 9: The Service

"Then I heard the voice of the Lord, saying, "Whom shall I send, and who will go for Us?"

- Luke 10:1-2 21

"So then, as we have opportunity, let us do good to everyone, and especially to those who are of the household of faith."

-Galatians 6:10

MY WHOLE LIFE HAS BEEN dedicated to serving God. It's been my calling, my purpose, and my passion. I've poured my heart into this path of service.

After graduating from California State University, I earned a Bachelor of Science in Health and Nutritional Science. My educational journey was just the beginning.

I went on to graduate from Bryman College and Long Beach Bible Institute/College. I received a Certificate in Ministry, which covered topics like Church and pulpit Etiquette, Altar Work, Officiating Weddings and funerals, Premarital and Post post-marital counseling, and even understanding and helping Battered and abused Women and children, and other biblical studies like hermeneutics, homiletics, apologetics, church administration, and other ministries biblical studies. I also attended the Mother Barbara McCoo Lewis School of Missionary Development.

In 1979, I proudly received my Aspiring Missionary License, followed by my Evangelist Missionary License in 1981. These licenses were important steps on my journey of service.

ELAINE BEVERLY ROBINSON WILLIAMS

I've been involved with various churches and ministries. I've served at Holy Mountain Church of God in Christ, Los Angeles, under the late Pastor Cleo M. Austin, 88th Street Temple Church of God in Christ, Los Angeles, California, under the late Bishop B. R. Benbow, and the current Pastor Anthony Williams, and the Greater Open Door Worldwide Ministry, Long Beach, California, under the leadership of Bishop, Dr. Garon Harden. I'm also a member of Sisters-in-Ministry under the leadership of Pastor Sonja Dawson of New Mount Calvary, Los Angeles, California, and Victory Outreach in Long Beach, California, His Nesting Place for unwed mothers, in Long Beach, California, a community that shares the same commitment.

Throughout the years, I've taken on many roles in my church family. I've been a Sunday School Secretary, Teacher, and Assistant Superintendent. I served as a Deaconess and President of the Cradle Row Auxiliary. I've even taken on responsibilities outside the church walls, serving as a District Field Representative for Sunday School and volunteering for Prison Ministry, Street Evangelism, Hospital Care Mission, and the Bereavement Committee. I'm an Intercessor, a Prayer Warrior, and a sidewalk Counselor for Unwed Mothers. Whenever there's a need, I'm there to serve.

My experiences regarding the outreach ministry at the Los Angeles Downtown – a place where it breaks the cycle of homelessness and poverty by stabilizing people in a safe and spiritual environment, connecting them to solutions, and walking with them on their journey with Pastor Sonja Dawson of Sisters-in Ministry. We got involved with individually praying for their immediate needs, providing some toiletries, distributing clothing, and sharing the gospel words of encouragement.

Outreach ministry is the practice of looking beyond yourself to the people around you and sharing the love of Christ as you serve and connect with your community. This doesn't require a big budget or a five-year plan. You can simply start with whatever is in your hand that you can offer to your neighbor.

Scripture is full of outreach examples where there was a need, and God's people got resourceful. There's the story of the crowd being fed by five loaves and two fish (Matthew 14). There's the time a group of friends figured out how to open up a roof to get their friend to Jesus (Mark 2). Throughout history, God has used the unlikely, the common, the unexpected. I would even dare to say that God delights in using the unexpected. We serve a God who is resourceful. And we reflect God's image.

His Nesting Place provides mothers and children a safe, loving home and church that instills the gospel and encourages change In hopes of transforming their lives and turning them into the God-fearing, hard-working, independent mothers that God has destined them to be. Along with this mission, some do not want to be mothers, so the act of encouraging them not to go to a clinic and do the unthinkable, I was one of the counselors who witnessed to them about God's love and encouraged them about the mission on the sidewalk and a lot of times we are doing this evangelism outside of the clinic.

Victory Outreach is an international church-oriented Christian ministry called to evangelize and discipline the world's hurting people with the message of hope and the plan of Jesus Christ. We would either go to a public location, streets (train station, mall), or door-to-door to share the Gospel. It was mostly done in downtown Long Beach on Friday evenings, called the twilight hours. The twilight hours were chosen because we were trying to reach the homeless, drug addicts, prostitutes, ex-prisoners, and alcoholics, and that was the time they were on the street.

God calls us to show patience, love, forbearance, kindness, and so on when talking to the people on the street. Showing kindness while we hand out gospel tracts as we walk up to them, prayerfully, to communicate the gospel. What they need to know is that Christ came in fulfillment of the promises to put sin to death, Satan to flight, and sin to rest. They need hope. Jesus calls us to make disciples. I agree that outreach serves a vital function, filling in a gap in access to services and helping those who face heightened barriers to care. That is fulfilling the ministry to Go ye therefore, and teach all nations, baptizing them in the name of the Father, and of the Son, and of the Holy Ghost: Matthew 28:19

When 911 happened, I was residing in Long Beach and was not able to drive to my church in Los Angeles, the 88th Street Temple church, so God opened a door for me to teach Sunday School at Pastor Leon Woods church across the street from where I lived. It was a wonderful experience to be chosen for this task.

In my professional life, I work as a Secretary at the United States Customs and Border Protection. But my true calling, my real passion, is in serving God and His people. It's been an incredible journey, and I'm grateful for every opportunity to make a difference.

Handling Travel authorizations, Vouchers, and Claims for all my fellow employees in Tactical Operations is a big part of what I do. I'm always ready to help whenever I'm needed, and my willingness to assist is something I take pride in.

I was also involved with the Export Control Unit, where I managed the Department of State Licenses like DSP – 5, DSP – 6, and DSP – 94 licenses. I use the database to search for information, read and review licenses, add comments, and even manage deletions. Once everything is sorted, I make sure to send the deleted and expired licenses to the Department of State.

This year, I stepped up by taking on an extra responsibility – the Combined Federal Campaign. I talked to my fellow employees, sharing important information about why contributing to charity foundations matters. I'm happy to say that our efforts paid off, resulting in over $9,000.00 in donations from the Tactical Operations unit.

Working well with my coworkers is important to me. I'm always up for participating in office activities, whether it's the Federal Women's Program Manager, Blacks in Government, Special Emphasis Programs, Blood drives, FEMA, or any other event. I'm also comfortable working with little or no supervision, and I make sure to meet deadlines even when things get busy.

My work is all about supporting the mission to protect our nation's borders. By helping CBP Officers and their managers, I play a role in keeping the public safe from terrorists and dangerous things. It's a responsibility I take seriously, and I approach it with vigilance, integrity, and professionalism.

I want to mention that I was elected as the secretary of the NTEU 111 executive office, which I'm proud of. It shows my commitment to our team and willingness to take on important roles.

My work combines managing important paperwork, stepping up to support charity efforts, and playing a role in keeping our nation safe. It's all about teamwork, dedication, and making a positive impact.

I am forever grateful to the Lord for the way my life has taken shape, filled with countless accomplishments and exciting experiences.

Chapter 10: My Testimony

"Thou you have made me see troubles, many, and bitter, you will restore my life again."

-Psalm 71:20

LET ME BEGIN BY SAYING, **"God has been good to me."**

I have been through some storms, rain, trials, and tribulations, but look at me now. I am a living testimony; I could have been dead and gone, but the Lord stepped in and made death behave. He did not have to let me live. God has been my all-in-all, my friend, my Lord.

I am glad to be in the service one more time

you have no idea what I have been through.

For your goodness and your mercy toward me, I give you praise.

Oh Lord, I give you praise – hallelujah, and, oh Lord, I bless your name.

Song

Oh Lord, I give you praise

And oh Lord, I bless your name

And I Lift my voice to say thank you

For your goodness

And your mercy

Toward Me

I Offer praise (repeat)

You are worthy of

Glory, Honor,

Worthy of all praise

For your goodness

And your mercy

Toward Me

I Offer Praise

For your goodness

And your mercy toward us (repeat, modulate)

We offer praise (repeat)

I HAVE SO MUCH TO BE thankful for, many blessings, and many open doors.

I thank God for his goodness toward me.

"And they overcame him by the blood of the Lamb and by the words of their testimony."

-Revelation 12:11

Lord, give me the wisdom to share my testimony.

I want to glorify God and praise God for being good to me.

I thank God for waking me up every day. I thank God for covering me with His blood.

I thank God for keeping me from dangers seen and unseen. I thank God for saving me and sanctifying me. Thank God for filling me with your precious Holy Ghost and placing me in the ministry.

In 2018, I was evicted after I returned from volunteering with FEMA deployment in Dallas, TX, where I had been voluntarily assisting with the aftermath of the major hurricanes Harvey, Irma, and Maria in 2017. To my surprise, I received a mere three-day notice to quit and vacate my residence. It was shocking as I had nothing in my hand to arrange for my living. At this time, I had to go through immense pain and struggle. But all I knew was that God was beside me. He would pull me through the odds, and once again, I'd live up to my standards. Thankfully, life flowed, and several good things came my way.

As I look back over my life from when the pandemic began until now, I can truly say that I have been a blessing and have a testimony.:

When I awoke on Easter Sunday, April 12, 2020, my head was spinning all around the room – an out-of-body experience. I could not stand up without falling. At that time, I did not know what was happening. I called my doctor, who instructed me to go directly to the emergency room and not drive my car. So, I ordered an Uber because I had no one to take me to the hospital. The Uber took me to Cedar Sinai Medical Center's emergency room. They admitted me to the triage and said my blood pressure was high and I could have had a stroke. So, I thank God that he gave me the strength to walk out of the house to the Uber car without falling, arriving at my destination without blackening out, and no harm was done when I was slipping in and out of consciousness. I was diagnosed with an elevated blood pressure of 196/121. I was given some medicine that made me vomit, and I was released with a BP medication. I thank God they did not admit me to the hospital when COVID was taken over all the hospital rooms.

During the pandemic, my place of employment favored me to telework from home. Thank you, Jesus. I give Him praise. On January 31, 2023, I spent 31 years with this company as a secretary office automation.

In September 2020, my health suffered another attack of an unpleasant diagnosis of breast cancer that metastasized to my lymphatic system underarm. So, I underwent multiple mammograms, biopsy, ultrasounds, ingested dyes, surgery, removal of the lump, chemotherapy, and radiation. I did not have anyone to take me to all those appointments, so I drove myself. I thank God for taking me back and forth with no accident. I live in La Puente, and my appointment was in Beverly Hills. One hour and 10 minutes ride, a 35-mile journey drive one way. It was God's grace that kept me through it all. So, I Thank God and praise Him, for he is worthy of it all.

The chemotherapy treatment left me with hair loss. My fingernails were discolored black, my fingers had nerve damage, and I am suffering today with painful neuropathy still in my fingers and toes and weakness in my bones.

Today, I can say that I am a cancer survivor.

During the covid pandemic, my place of employment required all employees to receive the covid vaccines as a preventative precaution for maintaining employment. I received my vaccination in March 2021 to avoid the infection. The vaccine left me with muscle cramps in my arms and legs, especially at the injection site.

Here I am chosen by God to proclaim His word and to shew forth his praise, holy ghost filled, Evangelist Missionary, ministering to others, laying on hands, watching others healed, exercising the gifts God placed on me, seeing the manifestation and evidence of God's grace, to see that I was the one who requires healing. I was the one sick and needing help. All kinds of thoughts were going through my head that the church believers would think I was not living up to part, perceived incorrectly, and inadequate as an Evangelist. Those were my thoughts. The Bible encouraged me by saying, "In this life, we shall have tribulation, but be of good cheer, for God has overcome them all. Today, I declare that God is bringing me through this. Thank God.

Several times, God could have snatched me out of this life/world:

1. An abscess burst in my right ear, resulting in loss of hearing.
2. Equilibrium/balance off
3. Falling off a wall, dislocating my shoulders
4. Falling off a bike
5. Crashing in a tree
6. Scarred up
7. I swallowed a needle that passed through my intestine.
8. Stab with an icepick by a family member – younger sister (Marcia)
9. Eyes blacken and choked by another sister (Betty)
10. Hot iron burnt in my head by an ex-husband (Bruce)
11. The pressure cooker exploding in my face and shoulder has the scars to prove it.
12. Several car accidents left me with chronic pains, head injury, crushed ribs, whiplash, dislocated disks in the spinal cord, neck to lower back, fractured hip, torn ligaments, and pulled muscles.
13. Twisted ankles.
14. Fell twenty-five flights of stairs
15. Bruised, bang up, broken
16. Diabetes
17. Breast cancer
18. Cholesterol high
19. Abnormal blood pressure – hypertension

20. Neuropathy

These are not the only times I could have left this life, sleeping in a grave. So, I thank God. I thank God for keeping me alive.

God still has His powerful hands upon my life when, on May 03, 2021, there was a terrible car accident., that totaled my car. God, he protected me from death. I believe they pronounced me dead at the scene, and I woke up in the trauma center of Pomona Valley Hospital. This accident happens Two days before my 62nd birthday. My car brakes would not stop while approaching a major intersection whose light was turning 'red.' I swerve toward the sidewalk to prevent entering the intersection.

Instead, the car kept going; it jumped the sidewalk, and I did not know there was an iron bar hidden in the tree which stopped me from entering the gas station on my right while the car was still moving and I was pressing on the brakes for the car to stop. The car still did not stop. The sign in the tree, flip my car over into the street, upside down. The windows and roof glass broke, and the hospital kept picking glass and stopping blood out of my head, rushing me for Catscan, MRI, and chest X-ray. I was diagnosed with a head injury that affected my speech and handwriting, a terrible headache, and hair loss. I could not understand what I was writing. My speech was slurred. I was also diagnosed with crushed ribs that left me bent over, unable to stand up straight, using a walker and, with helpers, a wheelchair. My hip was fractured, and it is still difficult to rotate upstairs.

I thank God for allowing all the first responders to rush to help me: my car doors had to be pried off to remove me from upside down by firemen, my seat belt was cut to stop the crushing of my ribs, sheriffs lifted me out of my car unto paramedics, paramedics used their siren ambulance to whisk me away on the freeway to rush me to hospital, nurses were ready to swift me off to that x-ray. I slept all day in the hospital, where they intermittently woke me up so I couldn't slip into a coma. I guess the tow truck was there to move my car out of the street to the tow yard.

I thank God that the airbag did not deploy because it would have broken my neck and suffocated me; I thank God the car did not ignite and blow me up in it. I thank God the glass did not penetrate deep into my brain. I thank God that I did not enter that intersection, nor the gas station, because I would not be standing here to give you my testimony. I thank God that my car did not hit anyone or another car.

I am so grateful. I have seen this same kind of accident with no survivors.

I have read many reports of accidents like mine, but they did not make it. I am thankful to be alive today.

I thank God for His Supernatural powers that saved me that day from dying. Every day, I wake up, and I am grateful to see that day. I am walking better but am still relying on the walker to hold me up. The headaches that I am experiencing today feel like something is lifting my head off without giving me some anesthesia to stop it. I am alive today because God kept me, and he left me here to declare God's glory and to shew forth his praises. I have no sad story to tell you. I am so grateful to be still here. Jesus showed up at the scene of this accident. No other cars were involved. The sheriff did not drag me off for drunk driving. I thank God for what could have happened and what didn't happen. I got hindered from writing this testimony by shutting down my computer, and I couldn't type it out or log in to my computer.

While I have many people watching, waiting for my demise to see if I will make it out of the year 2021, I thank God it is September 29, 2023. I thank God it has been two years since the accident. Thank God. I know God today as a healer because he is improving me. I thank him for covering and protecting me with miracles, signs, and wonders, showing Himself mighty/strong right before my eyes, for there is none like him.

Chapter 11: Tragedy

———

"The Spirit of the Lord GOD is upon me; because the LORD hath anointed me to preach good tidings unto the meek; he hath sent me to bind up the brokenhearted, to proclaim liberty to the captives, and the opening of the prison to them that are bound;

2 To proclaim the acceptable year of the LORD, and the day of vengeance of our God; to comfort all that mourn;

3 To appoint unto them that mourn in Zion, to give unto them beauty for ashes, the oil of joy for mourning, the garment of praise for the spirit of heaviness; that they might be called trees of righteousness, the planting of the LORD, that he might be glorified."

-Isaiah 61:1-3

TRAGEDY IS A MERCILESS force that has the power to turn lives upside down in the blink of an eye. I realized it came as an uninvited guest, filling the room with sorrow and despair. Whether it be the loss of a loved one, a traumatic accident, or even personal failure, tragedy has no hesitation when it comes to reshaping my world. The emotional toll it took on me was profound and long-lasting.

It engulfed me in a cloud of grief and confusion, leaving scars that may never fully heal. This altered my perception of myself and the world around me; suddenly, I questioned everything I once believed to be true. But in every torment it brought, it also brought solace, revealing my hidden strengths - resilience and courage I had never imagined I possessed.

As I arrived back home after volunteering at FEMA, I discovered that all the rent payments I had made were returned to me via my mailbox. So, I had to use the refunded amount to sustain myself in various hotels and motels near my workplace until I ran out of money.

In the midst of my desperation and homelessness, I thought of sleeping in my car, only to be informed by an officer that it was not permissible to do so in the parking lot. So, I resided out of the trunk of my car, with only a change of clothes and other essential items. At this point, I reached out to my sister, Shirley, and her husband, seeking refuge in their home. Regrettably, my brother-in-law expressed reluctance to accommodate me. However, after some deliberation, my sister Shirley persuaded him to extend their hospitality toward me. These series of events not only presented me with significant challenges but also compelled me to confront the harsh realities of life. Despite the difficulties, I remained resilient and resourceful, seeking alternative means to sustain myself until I could secure a stable living arrangement. One night, I was leaving for the parking lot, burdened by running out of money and my gas tank was low. Unfortunately, I couldn't get to my sister Shirley's home as she lived far away. At this time, I desperately needed help. I was calling to God to send someone my way. Thankfully, He did. A kind friend came to my rescue, offering me a one-night stay at a motel so that I could make it to work the following day.

After that day, I went on living with my sister. Initially, I was not entrusted with the house keys, so I had to wake up at 3:30 am in the morning and get dressed before the family departed for work. The same routine was to be followed coming back home.

One day, after enduring a grueling two-hour traffic jam, I had to use the bathroom urgently. At this time, my sister and her family were at home, yet they claimed not to have heard my pleas to knock on the door and call. They left me to squirm uncomfortably on the porch for an extended period before finally allowing me to enter. This was coupled with my frequent instances of arriving at work at 4 a.m. and dozing off in my car in the parking lot before checking in at work at 8 a.m. when I was expected to report to work. It left me feeling frustrated. I wanted to say a lot but resisted because I was in need.

Deep down, I knew I was relying on their charity, thus suppressing my anger. They were well aware that I had no money and no place to go and still treated me miserably. This left a deep void inside me. I always felt like I was constantly rejected. And as the years went on, it took a toll on me. Quite unfortunately, to this day, I continue to experience a sense of rejection because of this. I feel that I deserve to be treated much better. But it wasn't the only thing that I endured. I endured all of the following and still came out victorious;

The murder of one of my twin brothers – Donovan, who was shot in his back, running from gunmen in his home.

Murder of my brother – Alphonso Jr., who was shot in the head while he was sitting in his wife's car.

Death of my father – Alphonso Sr., due to a brain aneurysm in his wife – Julie's lap.

Death of my six-month-old son – Denzel Wesley. It was a Sudden death of an infant at the babysitter's.

Death of My Stepmom – Julie at the age of 93years

Death of my Aunt – Mae at the age of 95 years

Unfortunately, both my stepmom and aunt died in the same week, one day apart. The good thing is, I know these were my testing times. God was testing my patience and how much pain I could endure.

My faith was challenged, forcing me to question my beliefs and seek solace in God's comfort and guidance.

"There hath no temptation taken hold of you but such as is common to man. But God is faithful; He will not suffer you to be tempted beyond that which ye are able to bear, but with the temptation will also make a way to escape, that ye may be able to bear it."

-1 Corinthians 10:13

"When you pass through the waters, I will be with you; and through the rivers, they shall not overwhelm you; when you walk through fire you shall not be burned, and the flame shall not consume you."

-Isaiah 43:2

A Psalm of David. *"The Lord is my shepherd; I shall not want. He makes me lie down in green pastures. He leads me beside still waters. He restores my soul. He leads me in paths of righteousness for his name's sake. Even though I walk through the valley of the shadow of death, I will fear no evil, for you are with me; your rod and your staff, they comfort me. You prepare a table before me in the presence of my enemies; you anoint my head with oil; my cup overflows. Surely goodness and mercy shall follow me all the days of my life, and I will dwell in the house of the Lord forever."* Amen.

-Psalms 23:1-6

The Bible mentions numerous tragic events like Job's trials, Moses's exile, and Jesus's crucifixion. I took inspiration from these stories. They taught me that there is hope for reconciliation and renewal even in the face of overwhelming tragedy.

God is the sailor of the ship of my life, and trusting His plan and finding strength in His love can make it easier to navigate complex situations. Today, I am convinced that tragedy served as a catalyst for spiritual transformation and deepening my relationship with God.

"And we know that for those who love God, all things work together for good, for those who are called according to his purpose."

-Romans 8:28 ESV

"For I consider that the sufferings of this present time are not worth comparing with the glory that is to be revealed to us."

-Romans 8:18 ESV

"Blessed be the Lord, who daily bears us up; God is our salvation. Selah"

TRIUMPHING THROUGH LIFE'S TRIALS: GOD'S GUIDING HANDS

-Psalm 68:19 ESV

"In this, you rejoice, though now for a little while, if necessary, you have been grieved by various trials."

-1 Peter 1:6-9 ESV

"For we do not want you to be unaware, brothers, of the affliction we experienced. For we were so utterly burdened beyond our strength that we despaired of life itself."

-2 Corinthians 1:8 ESV / 8 helpful votes

"Then the Lord knows how to rescue the godly from trials, and to keep the unrighteous under punishment until the day of judgment."

-2 Peter 2:9 ESV / 7 helpful votes

May my last days on earth be my best days, and to make heaven my home. Amen.